Beautiful
Minnesota

Beautiful
Minnesota

Text by Robin Will

First Edition November, 1978
Published by Beautiful America Publishing Company
4720 S.W. Washington, Beaverton, Oregon 97005
Robert D. Shangle, Publisher

Library of Congress Cataloging in Publication Data
Will, Robin, 1948-
   Beautiful Minnesota
   1. Minnesota—Description and travel—1951-
—Views. I. Title.
F607.W54   917.76'04'3   78-26080
ISBN 0-915796-61-9
ISBN 0-915796-60-0 pbk.

PHOTO CREDITS

CONTENTS

Beautiful America Publishing Company

The nation's foremost publisher of quality color photography.

CURRENT BOOKS

Utah, Texas, Alaska, Hawaii, Georgia, Arizona, Montana, Michigan, Colorado,
Washington, Minnesota, California, California II, No. California, No. California II,
So. California, San Francisco, Oregon II, British Columbia, California Missions,
Western Impressions, Lewis & Clark Country.

FORTHCOMING BOOKS IN 1979

Massachusetts, Pennsylvania, Maryland, Wisconsin, Kentucky, Florida, Illinois, Ohio,
Idaho, North Idaho, California Coast, Oregon Mountains, Nevada, New Mexico, Montana II,
Rocky Mountains, North Carolina, South Carolina, Virginia, Oklahoma, Michigan II,
Mississippi, Kentucky, Missouri.

1979 CALENDARS

Hawaii, Oregon, Colorado, California,
Michigan, Washington, Western America, Beautiful America.

Send for complete catalog, 50 ᶜ
Beautiful America Publishing Company
4720 S.W. Washington
Beaverton, Oregon 97005

BEAUTIFUL MINNESOTA

In the language of the Sioux, the word "minne-" means water, and "-sota" refers to the roiled and cloudy appearance of a stormy sky. The term "minnesota" has been translated in a variety of ways, but general opinion agrees that "land of sky-tinted waters" is as close as mere English can come to the meaning of the word. Seldom has a place been more aptly named. The geography of the state of Minnesota, and much of its character as well, have been formed in the crucible of water, weather and land which the Sioux recognized and named when they were the sole proprietors of the place.

To name a place like Minnesota for its waters requires no more than average powers of observation, but the Sioux went one better than that. "Sky-tinted" is the operational part of that definition. Water that is roiled and swirling like the clouds of a prairie storm is *water that moves.* Running water, set free after a winter's freeze, moving, working, shaping—that's the force that makes this country special. In naming Minnesota for flowing waters, the Sioux recognized something that has shaped the land and its people to this day: a restless, formative vitality and an orientation to nature.

It is hard, of course, to focus on the rivers and ignore the lakes, the more famous part of Minnesota's watery heritage. The state's automobile license plates claim ten thousand of them, and that figure is wildly conservative. Fifteen-thousand-plus is more like it, counting "any basin of ten or more acres, partially or completely filled with water." The rest are ponds, which do not count, and there are some swamps, which are really lakes that are farther along in their development, engaged in the process of filling themselves in and becoming dry land. But many of the lakes flow, just like rivers, and in the boundary chain particularly it's tough to distinguish between the lakes and the rivers that connect them. Minnesota offers the full spectrum where waterways are concerned.

The waterways meant transportation from man's earliest days in this country, and Minnesota's sufficiency thereof made it a frontier crossroads. Follow a great river to its source, and the likelihood of ending up in Minnesota is good. The St. Lawrence from the Atlantic, the Mississippi from the south, and the Red River from Hudson Bay (via Lake Winnipeg) all have sources in this country. Though the land is not particularly rugged as those things go, Minnesota might as well be the top of the world: water flows away from it in all directions. Minnesota is at the end of every road.

People have been taking advantage of Minnesota's position at the "center of the world" for as long as mankind has been traveling. Ancient mound-builders once roamed the woods and fished the lakes and streams, leaving their massive and enigmatic earthworks for later generations to ponder. More recent Indian tribes trapped and fished in the dark forests, and hunted buffalo on the plains in the south. A band of Vikings probably explored Minnesota in the 14th century, but other Europeans were slow to follow: missionaries and explorers came by way of the rivers in the 16th and 17th centuries. The voyageurs, French-Canadian adventurers and the grass-roots of the fur trade, plied the rivers and lakes in fragile birchbark canoes. Behind the voyageurs—up the same rivers—came settlers: farmers, loggers, millers. And everyone who passed through left their mark on the land in some way.

Two groups, however, left their marks not as much on the land as on the imagination: Vikings and voyageurs are both subjects of legends which shape the way Minnesotans think of themselves to this day. It is likely that Viking explorers visited Minnesota in the fourteenth century, traveling up the Red River from Lake Winnipeg. Evidence for this belief exists, and while it has never been totally accepted, neither has it ever been convincingly disproved. Minnesotans like the story, true or not, in part because so many of them have Scandinavian roots, and in part because it is such a good story. What Minnesota historians refer to carefully as "the Viking myth" adds to the image of the rugged, self-reliant and winter-proof outdoorsman. Minnesotans like to think of themselves in those terms.

The image of the voyageurs also looms large in the Minnesotans' sense of who they are. Traversing peaceful lakes and whitewater rivers in their fragile birchbark canoes, prevailing against incredible odds and deprivations, the voyageurs led lives of adventure, celebration and danger. Trade goods for the Indians came to Grand Portage in 90-pound bundles, and furs went out the same way . . . two or three bundles at a time, on the backs of voyageurs. Working when they had to and playing when they could, these hardy men seemed to inspire early writers, historians and explorers with their unquenchable spirit and their knowledge of this great new land. Today Minnesotans ply the same lakes in adaptations of the same craft: the canoes, instead of birchbark or pitch, are aluminum or fiberglass now, but a good portion of the wilderness is still there, and many of the lakes are the same, or nearly so. The voyageur spirit still lives in Minnesota.

Of course, between Minnesota's many waterways are bits of land, and it was land that American settlers were after. Behind the voyageurs were farmers, who knew that rivers guaranteed a means of getting their produce to market. Behind the farmers came loggers, for the forests of white pine, and millers who could use the power of the rivers to cut logs into lumber or grind wheat into flour. Minnesota was on the way to leading the nation in lumbering and wheat production when the rich iron range was discovered, exposing yet another facet in the complicated and energetic character of the territory.

Perhaps it's the tradition of the winter-proof Viking, or perhaps just the vitality of a people used to living close to nature, that makes Minnesota a center for winter sports. No matter what the reason, it's a good thing Minnesotans have discovered ways to enjoy their winter . . . there is so much winter to enjoy. Ice-fishing, hockey, skiing, snowmobiling, iceboating, dog-sledding, curling and snowshoeing bring well-bundled Minnesotans of all ages away from their firesides and out into winters of legendary duration and intensity. Instead of fighting the cold, Minnesotans celebrate it with spectacular winter carnivals, parades and such, and Bemidji and Hibbing take cold comfort from competition for the status of the nation's coldest city.

Today the Minnesota character spans the variety of its traditions and then some, as if tradition, like money in the bank, accrued compound interest. The wilderness-loving, outdoor-oriented aspect of Minnesotans is no surprise considering the variety of ways in which nature and geography offer their riches. And it's no surprise that conservation and appreciation of natural resources have been high priorities for years.

One wonders to what extent the other aspects of Minnesota owe themselves to this appreciation of things wild and free. The progressive cities, energetic industry, and some of the most productive and innovative agriculture in the world may well owe some of their stature in part to the fact that it is so easy here to return to the woods and the waters, soak up the silence, and get in touch with the forces that keep mankind running on an even keel. All in all, man needs to know that he is still in relationship with nature, and in Minnesota, nature makes offers, and issues demands, which are difficult to ignore.

There is no way a mere book can do justice to the splendor and variety to be found in Minnesota. The task of choosing five or six dozen scenes from the multitude of photogenic places in the state is staggering. To try to make our choices somehow representative of all there is to see would be a task to beggar the imagination. So we didn't try. We took another kind of approach—one which we heartily recommend—and *browsed* through the state, stopping here and there to look more closely at things we found interesting. We hope the results of our perusal of Minnesota—this volume of pictures and words—will bring the reader even a fraction of the delight we experienced in compiling it. It has been fun.

R.W.

(Preceding page) Trees cling to a rocky island in one of Minnesota's Boundary Lakes.

(Opposite) Autumn's chilly nights bring radiant colors to the woods in the North Shore area of Lake Superior.

(Right) Brilliant Canna blooms in profusion in Minnesota gardens.

(Below) Split Rock Lighthouse stands like a sentinel over the waters of Lake Superior.

(Following pages) High Falls—the highest in Minnesota—occur on Baptism Creek, on Lake Superior's north shore.

(Second following page, above) Colorful landscaping highlights the grounds of the state capitol in St. Paul.

(Below) Evening brings shadows and moody clouds to the rolling farmland north of Minneapolis.

(Third following page) Splashing waters build up spectacular mantles of ice on the rugged Lake Superior shoreline.

(Preceding pages) A profusion of wildflowers highlights this pastoral scene near Frontenac State Park.

(Left) A delicate rosebud unfolds in the Minnesota sunlight.

(Below) Wisconsin is on the left bank of the St. Croix, Minnesota on the right, in this view in Interstate State Park.

(Opposite) Many quiet coves punctuate the rocky Lake Superior shoreline.

(Opposite) A mixture of hardwoods and evergreens makes a colorful sight on the rocky banks of the St. Croix, one of the nation's truly ''wild'' rivers along most of its length.

(Right) Springtime's warm sun nurtures incredible floral variety.

(Below) Sunny solitude is one of the attractions of Paradise Beach lakeshore, in Cook County.

(Following page, above) Minnehaha Park, Minneapolis, is lush and verdant in mid-August.

(Following page, below) Clouds form a striking tapestry in the wide-open sky above Blue Mounds State Park.

(Second following page) Beaver Bay is a quiet inlet on the north shore of Lake Superior.

(Third following page) Sheer rock walls rise from the cold waters of Lake Superior at Palisade Head.

THE BOUNDARY

Minnesota, being a long, narrow state north to south, admits of no easy internal divisions. There is not much difference between the land in eastern Minnesota and the land in western Minnesota, because not many miles separate them; and as a result no such regions have ever been staked out on maps or in the public consciousness. However, Minnesotans do have a clear sense of North and South as geographic entities, and though there is some good-natured debate about where the line is drawn, the terms north and south have specific meanings to the native of Minnesota.

The term ''north'' applies in a general way to all the country north of the Twin Cities—about three-quarters of the state. Though this predominance of northernness might be confusing, Minnesotans use the term ''north'' in a specific sense. North simply means ''not-South,'' and South means that portion of the state which is a continuation of the Great Plains and the Corn Belt. That chunk of Plains, farmland of spectacular virtue, comprises one of the few natural physical regions in Minnesota . . . most of the rest tends, with charming ''monotony,'' to be lake-and-forest country, where recreation, logging and mining take place more often than farming. By that measure, Brainerd, the city closest to the geographical center of Minnesota, is considered northern; and even down in Pine City, well south of center, a radio station advertises itself as the ''Voice of the North.'' Bemidji and Grand Rapids are definitely northern cities—no one argues that—but there's still country north of that. The north-of-north cities of International Falls, Baudette, Warroad and the like are considered ''up on the Boundary,'' the border between the United States and Canada.

In the west, the International Boundary slices across an 80-mile expanse of The Valley—which immediately gives lie to the notion that ''they don't farm much in the north.'' The Red River of the North drains the dead-flat bottom of prehistoric Lake Agassiz, where special cold-climate adaptations of malting barley, sugar beets, and high-yield dwarf wheat regularly produce crops of astounding plenty. The sand ridge between Karlstad and Roseau was the shore of the ancient lake, and State Highway 11, roughly following the ridge, takes you from valley flatness into rolling, wooded land dotted with occasional muskeg or peat bogs. The highway duplicates the route of

(Preceding page, above) The golden tones of autumn get a boost from the dazzling reflections in the waters of the Gooseberry River.
(Preceding page, below) The majestic dome of St. Paul Cathedral rises near the state capitol grounds in St. Paul.

an early Indian war road which was later used by fur traders and early settlers. The town of Warroad, on Lake of the Woods, commemorates this history in its name.

Outside of The Valley, lumber was king on the boundary for as long as it lasted. Pursuing the valuable white pine, loggers combed the north woods, building towns which boomed while the timber held out and declined when the woodsmen moved on. Working in the winter, when the frozen earth made it easier to skid logs out of the swampy forests, loggers took millions of board feet of lumber out of these woods between 1880 and the 1920s. Though the great boom is gone and reforestation is the word in much of this region, the lumber and paper industries still contribute heavily to the area's payrolls. Second-growth timber, mostly birch, ash and other hardwoods that don't mind getting their feet wet, now mask the scars loggers left on the land, and prepare the soil for another round of pine later on. The traveler who wants to see it the way it was should detour to the wildlife refuge on the road between Roseau and the border town of Pinecreek. There, in the midst of 50,000 acres of untrammeled wilderness, it's possible to observe deer, moose and a variety of waterfowl in their native habitat.

The town of Warroad is situated on the southern shore of Lake of the Woods, offering the only American access to the lake's islands and that geographical oddity, the Northwest Angle. The Angle is a piece of American land on the Canadian side of Lake of the Woods. It became American territory through the treaty that granted American independence from the British, back in the days when it was believed that the Mississippi River lay somewhere west of the big lake. It doesn't, and the line that was supposed to be drawn from the northwest corner of Lake of the Woods directly westward to the Mississippi was drawn south to the 49th parallel instead. The result is a small lobe of land accessible only by water—or ice—from the American ''mainland,'' or by Canadian highway. The community of Penasse is there, and the Angle's main activity aside from tourism is logging in the wintertime when the spongy ground is frozen.

Beyond Warroad and south of Lake of the Woods is the hamlet of Williams, gateway to Beltrami Island State Forest. Another example of Minnesota's interest in conservation, the 445,500-acre forest is the home of one of the largest herds of caribou in the United States. Blueberries grow here in abundance, relishing the moisture in the landscape which alternates between pine hills and peat bogs. Bears grow here in abundance, too, relishing the blueberries. Williams is also the home of Lady Slipper Rest, a wayside where three kinds of the state flower may be seen.

(Following pages) This is the lowest of several waterfalls on the Gooseberry River, on Lake Superior's north shore.

From Baudette eastward, State 11 runs alongside the beautiful Rainy River, which flows from Rainy Lake into Lake of the Woods, thence to Hudson Bay. So peaceful that it resembles a narrow lake along most of its length, the river nevertheless gets rambunctions in two places: at Manitou Rapids, where it is forced through a narrow, rocky gorge, and again at International Falls.

Just west of International Falls is The Grand Mound, a massive burial mound from a prehistoric Indian culture named Laurel Indians for the small town nearby. An excellent interpretive center outlines what is known about the culture, which managed to build the Grand Mound and four others a short distance from the river more than 500 years ago. If numbers impress, Grand Mound is 325 feet in circumference and 45 feet high, while the four lesser ones have about 50-foot diameters and are four feet tall.

A different kind of impression is gathered by standing among the large, grass-covered bumps in the earth, watching the peaceful Rainy River slide past and listening to the wind blow through the nearby trees. Man's progress comes to nothing in such places: it is the same river, the same wind, that whispered and roared in the days when the mounds were new. Their mute antiquity engenders a sense of awe and introspection.

Not all of the border country is accessible by automobile. East of International Falls is Voyageurs National Park, and east of the park is Boundary Waters Canoe Area. It is possible to follow the boundary lakes and rivers clear to Grand Portage, on the shore of Lake Superior about 200 miles away. If you do that, you'll be retracing the route of the celebrated French-Canadian voyageurs, who for a century and a half used these interconnected waterways as a highway for the fur trade.

Though the colorful voyageur is gone, the land and the waters through which he traveled are still there. Deep, clear lakes reflect the blue of the sky while dark stands of pine cast deep shadows at the water's edge. Slipping silently through the waters in a canoe, the traveler is likely to surprise a bald eagle on his hunting trip, or an osprey with a fish clutched in its claws. Or the paddler may be startled by the other-worldly cry of a loon at twilight, the weird, manic laughter suddenly booming across the quiet water. Taking advantage of the canoe's silence, it's possible to get quite close to deer, bear, moose, and smaller animals as they come down to the water to drink.

Voyageurs National Park consists mainly of the Kabetogama Peninsula and the waters that surround it. In fact, Kabetogama barely misses being an island: it owes its status as a peninsula to a slender isthmus that moors it to the mainland on its west end. Its shoreline is ragged with inlets and bays. On the north is Rainy Lake, on the south is Kabetogama Lake, and on the east is the narrow, island-dotted strait which connects these two with Namakan Lake. As if all that water was not enough, Kabetogama Peninsula has lakes in its interior as well, accessible only by footpath through the forested hills.

The interior lakes provide an opportunity to practice another voyageur skill: the *portage.* It means carrying your canoe and all your gear from one body of water to the next. Some of the portage trails between here and Lake Superior are well over two hundred years old, having been in continuous use since the beginnings of recorded history in these parts.

Whatever effort is required of the modern voyageur, the interior of the peninsula makes it worthwhile. As in the rest of the boundary territory, logging began on the Kabetogama Peninsula in the 1880s. However, a hardy stand of second-growth timber keeps the streams and lakes clear and provides food and shelter for a variety of wildlife. In the uplands aspen, birch, balsam, spruce and maple grow in abundance. Boggy areas left by Ice Age glaciers provide footing for dense stands of black spruce, white cedar, ash and tamarack trees. Moose are seen occasionally, and white-tailed deer are common in the park. Campers are routinely and strenuously warned about the black bears, and the area also shelters some of the few remaining timber wolves in the United States. Smaller animals—mink, weasel, beaver, bobcat, rabbits and such— are abundant; fishing is good in the lakes and streams, and dozens of varieties of migratory or year-round waterfowl call the park their home.

Voyageurs National Park is one of the nation's newest, and development is proceeding slowly and cautiously. The intent is to keep the internal combustion engine out of the park interior—to keep these silent lakes and woodlands, enlivened only by the wild cry of the loon and the occasional splash of fish jumping, from being overrun by the glut of automobiles that pollute and plague some of our other national parks. The land will be preserved not only for the people who visit . . . in the long run, human convenience will likely be less of a consideration than preservation of the native animals and trees, with humans being admitted insofar as they don't disturb the ''original inhabitants.''

Directly east of Voyageurs National Park is Superior National Forest, which occupies most of Minnesota's Arrowhead region, from the border south to the north shore of Lake Superior. Within the National Forest, Boundary Waters Canoe Area is a wilderness preserve for canoeing, camping and backpacking. Serene lakes, whitewater rivers, waterfalls and rapids continue in an unbroken chain through the dark north woods. This is another area where it's not hard to feel the ghosts of the

(Following page) The Temperance River has carved itself a deep and shady gorge in the bedrock of the North Shore country.

31

voyageurs around you . . . relics of these early-day adventurers have been found in the still waters below rapids, evidence of canoes lost long ago on trading expeditions when some doughty boatman decided to shoot the rapids rather than go around. Portages today are well-marked and canoeists are urged to use them, lest difficult rapids or unexpected waterfalls end their journey prematurely.

This is grand country. In some places, the lakes are so large a canoeist can lose his bearings, while others are still pools or narrow, natural channels. Sometimes the lakes are separated by narrow necks of land, compelling a portage of a few rods or a mile. One unexpected bonus for the watchful traveler is the legacy of some prehistoric artists: pictographs can be found on rocks that overhang the water. The Chippewa were artists, and where they could reach from their canoes, they painted the objects that were familiar to them: suns, moons, men, moose, loons, pelicans and such, with a mixture of hematite and fish oil.

Continuing eastward, the canoeist will eventually reach Height of Land Portage, between North Lake and South Lake. It's a landmark because waters separate there, some flowing north and west to drain into Hudson Bay, and some flowing east to Lake Superior, the St. Lawrence River and the Atlantic Ocean. Some 20-30 miles farther on—*downstream,* this time—is the site of Ft. Charlotte, and the head of the Grand Portage trail. The trail, bypassing a particularly rugged portion of the Pigeon River, leads a scenic nine miles to the reconstructed stockade at Grand Portage, on the shore of Lake Superior.

Few people will ever make the whole trip from International Falls to Grand Portage—or vice-versa—in the tracks of the voyageurs. Such a trip does not fit with ease into the average summer vacation, nor the average lifestyle: not everyone *wants* to spend weeks in the solitude of still waters and deep forests. But those who enjoy the soul-stretching experience of the world's wild and free places will rejoice in this pristine stretch of running water, for whatever time they can spare.

(Preceding page, above) Sunrise blazes a shining path across the early-morning stillness of Lake Superior.
(Preceding page, below) This graceful bridge arches over a stream in Minnehaha Park, Minneapolis, near Hiawatha Golf Course.

VIKINGLAND

South of the Boundary country, there is still plenty of Minnesota that is considered northern, and several areas with strong regional identities: the ''north'' designation does not even hint at the variety and richness one finds there.

In the northwest, Minnesota is bordered by the Red River of the North—so-called on maps so nobody will confuse it with the Texas-Oklahoma Red River. This Red River drains a valley 80 miles wide, which was once the bed of prehistoric Lake Agassiz. Dead-flat, deeply fertile and well-watered, the land is given to agriculture, and the reports of crops from this area resemble an agricultural Paul Bunyan story. If Paul had had a brother who was a farmer, chances are he would have tilled the earth in The Valley, growing sugar beets, barley and grain that yield half again as much per acre as the national average.

Lakes are the main thing all over northern Minnesota, in one form or another, because most of the land either was a lake once, or is one right now. It is the nature of lakes, scientists tell us, to fill themselves up over the centuries with algae and vegetation until they become dry land. A great deal of northern Minnesota is represented on maps as swampland—lakes well advanced in the process of filling themselves in and becoming meadows and forests. And the border of the Red River Valley is marked by a beach where the waters of Lake Agassiz once lapped on prehistoric shores. It can be seen at Buffalo River State Park, between Moorhead and Hawley; in the north outside of Roseau, and as a general line in-between. This particular beach now languishes some 40 miles from the nearest water, and only the Red River remains to drain the basin.

The Red River sometimes seems to remember its heritage as a lake, and occasionally when rains are heavy it reverts to type, leaving its banks and, with nothing in the flat landscape to stop it, inundating miles of farmland.

The western portion of north Minnesota is known as Vikingland—for a couple of reasons. One is that the area was heavily populated with Scandinavian immigrants at one time, and today the names on rural mailboxes suggest that a great many families still trace their origins to Nordic stock. The other reason is that there exists a sizeable body of evidence to indicate that in 1362, this country was explored by Norsemen who were searching for settlers who had abandoned a colony in West Greenland.

(Following page, above) The Minneapolis skyline reveals a prosperous and growing city.
(Following page, below) A lone box elder stands on a tall-grass prairie at Glacial Lakes State Park.

Plenty of controversy exists on the subject. Some experts feel that the Kensington Runestone, discovered in 1898 by a Swedish immigrant farmer, was probably carved in about 1897 and hidden where it wouldn't be too hard to find. Others, perhaps not so expert, but definitely enthusiastic, feel the Kensington Runestone and some other discoveries make an airtight case for the argument that Vikingland, Minnesota style, is the site of the first European exploration of our continent, and thus is the "birthplace of America." Other discoveries—Viking relics like mooring stones and ancient battle-axes, add an intriguing ambiguity to the evidence.

The facts of the matter may be ambiguous, but there is no question about the impact the "Viking Myth" has had on public imagination in Minnesota. The Kensington Runestone even went to the New York World's Fair in 1964-65 . . . doing nothing to resolve the arguments about its origin, but bringing more attention than ever to Minnesota's claim as the birthplace of the nation. A Grant County farmer took a different approach to the runestone controversy, and carved his own runic inscriptions on a heart-shaped stone, insisting until his death that his wasn't the *only* phony runestone in the state. But one way or another, all Minnesotans relate to the story of early Viking explorations in the Valley. Most have adopted a good-natured neutrality about it, feeling that the Viking Myth is as much a part of the state's mystique as is Paul Bunyan—and you don't hear anybody questioning the authenticity of Paul Bunyan.

It is possible to take more or less the same route the Vikings took through The Valley on their trek from Hudson Bay, beginning at Noyes on the U.S.-Canadian border and traveling south. In the 14th century the floor of the Red River Valley would have been waist-deep in grass. Today it is plowed and planted with a variety of cash and feed crops, the flat horizon interrupted by monolithic structures of grain elevators, silos and the like. At one time some farmers here bragged that they could plow a single furrow seven or eight miles long in a straight line across the valley floor. That was back in the days when the railroads owned the land, and barons like James J. Hill presided over farms measured in square miles. Today the holdings are somewhat smaller.

State Highway 75 runs the length of the Red River Valley, either closely or exactly paralleling the old Pembina Trail, and early trade route, and before that, an Indian trail. Along this trail creaking oxcarts carried furs and trade goods to St. Paul and other ports, from the 1840s until they were replaced by railroads. The oxcart

(Preceding page) Morning mist hovers above a lake in the Boundary Waters Canoe Area.

38

trail has been commemorated in places like Old Crossing Treaty Wayside, about eight miles west of Red Lake Falls, where the trail's ruts may still be seen.

The possibility of Viking exploration in this area is reaffirmed by relics which suggest the 14th-century explorers used this same Pembina Trail. A Viking fire-steel was found in Climax by a farmer digging a posthole, and about a mile outside of Climax, a landslide after a heavy rain exposed an ancient Norse ceremonial halberd. It's an efficient-looking weapon which combines a spear point and an axe-blade on a long handle.

Then there is the business of the mooring stones. From Canada's Lake Winnipeg as far south as Kensington, curious drilled-out stones have been found on lake shores. They are identical to the stones Norwegian boatmen have used for centuries to secure their boats. At Big Cormorant Lake, 300 feet from the present lake on an earlier shoreline are three large granite boulders, each with a drilled hole about nine inches deep and an inch wide.

Skeptics claim they were drilled for some other purpose than anchoring Viking boats. Like anchoring log booms, for instance (though no logging has ever been done here). Another interpretation would have it that the stones were drilled as a preliminary to dynamiting to clear the land (though the stones—with holes—have been known for about 100 years, and dynamite in these parts was rare at the time the holes must have been drilled).

Believers claim that no other explanation fits as well as the obvious one: the mooring stones were left by a party of Norse explorers in the mid-1300s. Four such stones exist in the area east of Moorhead, and another has been found outside of Kensington, not far from the site where the famous runestone was discovered. Farther east, two more stones were found, including one on Lake Osakis, which drains into the Mississippi via the Sauk River. The mooring stones, scattered as they are, seem more difficult to explain away than some of the other Viking evidence.

It wouldn't be a tour of Minnesota without a stop at Itasca State Park, the source of the Mississippi River. Seven men claimed to have found the source of the Big Muddy before Henry Rowe Schoolcraft discovered Itasca in 1833. At this point, Big Muddy is neither big nor muddy: casually-placed stepping stones at the outlet of the lake enable tourists who are so inclined—and most of them are—to cross the shallow, clear-flowing stream with a hop, skip and a jump. Itasca State Park also has Indian burial mounds within its 32,000 acres, and enormous stands of virgin forest.

(Following page, above) Hardwood trees crowd close to shore in this typical Minnesota lake scene. (Following page, below) This colorful floral display is in a greenhouse at the Arboretum in Como Park, St. Paul.

(Preceding page) Summertime's low water relieves some of the violence of the Dalles of the Kettle River, typically an area of rough whitewater.

(Opposite) Winter's snow lies drifted deep and soft under the Minnesota pines.

(Right) A quiet pond supports delicate water lilies.

(Below) The St. Louis River winds through a rocky gorge in Carlton County.

(Following pages) Evening's last rays of sun lend a moody note to the landscape of southeast Minnesota's farming country.

(Second following page, above) The change in seasons brings a splash of color to the trees along the Kettle River.

(Second following page, below) Fluffy clouds provide their own dimension to this field of newly-mown hay in Aitkin County.

(Third following page) Slender, white-trunked birches crowd the shore of McDougal Lake.

(Preceding pages) The Mississippi River is a clear and startling blue at John Latch State Park.

(Left) Several varieties of lilies reward the efforts of Minnesota gardeners, and delight passersby.

(Below) The Upper Falls of the Gooseberry River show the water coloration from nearby Tamarack or peat bogs.

(Opposite) Minnesota's windswept sky backlights this grove of trees on the shore of Mille Lacs Lake.

(Opposite) The lower falls of the Brule River whip the water to angry foam before it joins Lake Superior.

(Right) Roses provide a visual feast in a shaded Minnesota garden.

(Below) The pure white trunks of the birches lend a slightly eerie tone in this shady grove at Itasca State Park.

(Following page, above) Trees along this shoreline drive take on brilliant hues in autumn.

(Following page, below) Torrential Minnehaha Falls plunges over a cliff and crashes to the stones below.

(Second following page) Early morning's still waters provide a striking reflection at one of the boundary lakes.

(Third following page) Fall color is a signal that winter is on the way in the boundary lakes country.

Schoolcraft claimed to have coined the name Itasca from the Latin term *veritas caput,* the words for *truth* and *head* or *source.* However, the origin of the name is a point of contention: Chippewa legend has it that the beautiful daughter of Hiawatha, Itaska, or I-tesk-ka, was carried away to the region of darkness by the ruler of the underworld, and the Mississippi was started by the tears she shed. More recent legend claims the great river had its beginning when Babe, Paul Bunyan's blue ox, tipped over a water tank in a logging camp . . . also a picturesque story, but it doesn't go far to explain the name.

However it began, Itasca and the Mississippi make up only a small portion of the total lakes and waterways in north-central Minnesota. Bemidji is in the heart of lake country, and not far from the edge of Chippewa National Forest. While places like Itasca get all the attention, it's possible to sneak off the beaten track and enjoy the quiet and solitude of uncrowded woods and waters in places like the Paul Bunyan State Forest. North Central Minnesota advertises itself as the home of the "fifth season" of the year, claiming that the mild and sunny Indian summers are more spectacular here than elsewhere. It's a hard point to argue. And when the snow lies deep, snowmobiles still provide a means for the warm-blooded to enjoy the wilderness.

Fans of geographic distinctions may appreciate a visit to another Continental Divide, clearly marked north of Bemidji at Buena Vista, an explorer campground and historic Indian trail site. The waters of Lake Julia flow north to Hudson Bay, while the waters from adjacent Little Turtle Lake drain towards the Gulf of Mexico. Enjoying such fine access by water, it's not surprising that this spot held special significance to early Indians.

(Preceding page, above) This peaceful farm scene is in Aitkin County.
(Preceding page, below) St. Paul's skyline rises dramatically from the waterfront.

THE RANGE AND THE ARROWHEAD

Two other areas of "northern" Minnesota have established strong regional identities, both defined in one sense or another by the scenery they have to offer. One is The Range, and the other is the Arrowhead, the triangular piece of land between Superior's north shore and the border.

Elsewhere in the United States, reference to the range would likely mean high, rolling grasslands, but in Minnesota the term means only one thing: the iron mining country of the Cuyuna, Vermilion and Mesabi iron ranges. At one time only the biggest and richest—the Mesabi—was entitled to be called *the* range, but lately the distinctions have become blurred and the name has begun to apply to all three of the districts, concentrated as they are in the same general area of northwestern Minnesota.

As early as 1865, significant amounts of iron were discovered in the area around Vermilion Lake, but Minnesotans weren't impressed. They were convinced that there was gold in those hills, and they had little time to spare for iron. But the gold deposits didn't amount to much, and within another generation priorities had been switched: by the turn of the century, Minnesota was a leader in the production of iron ore. The range towns of Hibbing, Virginia, Chisolm and a host of others grew up almost overnight, some prospering and others eventually waning as local ore pockets ran out. As some of the high-grade ore deposits were exhausted, Minnesota's economy began to slump, but the recent discovery of ways to process taconite, a plentiful lower-grade iron ore, has kept wheels turning and furnaces blasting in The Range.

The Range today is a combination of forested hills, peaceful lakes—and iron mines. Hibbing is the home of the Hull-Rust-Mahoning Mine, the world's largest open-pit iron mine. President Calvin Coolidge, in characteristic understatement, once commented that the mine was "a pretty big hole." In actuality, anything a person can say about Hull-Rust-Mahoning turns out to be an understatement. There is no use to scout for better superlatives, or to wring descriptive phrases from exhausted vocabularies: the big mine outdoes all attempts to describe it. In the cold, blue light of a Minnesota winter morning, when everything is lightly dusted with snow, the "big

(Following page) Trees and lichens cling to the rocks above the waters of Lake Superior.

hole'' and others like it take on an awesome, other-world appearance. Up in Ely, it's possible to see iron mining from another perspective: the Tower-Soudan State Park offers an underground tour of a conventional mine, a half-mile below the surface of the earth.

These mines, while they may not qualify for the title of natural beauty, are certainly landmarks and monuments in a sense to the ability of man to alter his environment. These mines—and the progress of the mining industry in general—are compelling Minnesotans to ask themselves some hard questions about their businesses and their environment. Answers do not come easily.

Beyond The Range to the east is the Arrowhead district, and the Superior National Forest. This district, named for its triangular shape, is defined by the Boundary Waters Canoe Area and the Canadian border on the north, and by Lake Superior on the south. The Arrowhead's principal city is Duluth, a major seaport since the completion of the St. Lawrence Seaway to the Atlantic. Duluth is the world's largest inland seaport, handling shipments of iron ore and taconite, lumber, grain and other products for the world market. However, just a short drive from the purposeful hum of business in Duluth's seaport, the great north woods begin in earnest. Arrowhead country contains untouched wilderness, developed vacation and resort areas, and the spectacular north shore drive—one of the nation's most scenic areas.

Thousands and millions of years ago, when Minnesota was a playground for glaciers, and before that, when this part of the country was the bed of an ancient sea, the land was more or less flat. As the land rose and volcanic action caused the earth's crust to fold (creating the huge dip that was to become Lake Superior) the Arrowhead country became a high and relatively flat plateau. Ravages of glacial ice, followed by torrential meltwaters, eroded great gashes across the face of this plateau, which have softened through time to become the rugged, hilly country that is seen today. Evidence is everywhere of the deep layers of underlying stone which have been exposed by the cutting action of running water. The result is land of charm and ruggedness, with deep river gorges and stone bluffs overlooking the great inland sea that is Lake Superior.

With the exception of several bustling commercial and pleasure harbors, preservation efforts have guaranteed that much of this country would look familiar to the voyageurs of the old days, if any were to come through. The north boundary of

(Preceding page, above) Grand Portage Bay features a reconstructed Northwest Company fur trading post at Grand Portage National Monument.

(Preceding page, below) A crop of sunflowers blooms under a clear sky on this southeastern Minnesota farm.

the United States at this point is the Pigeon River, which churns itself into furious white water at the bottom of its deep and rocky gorge. The river was named for flocks of passenger pigeons that were formerly found in the area. Several waterfalls along the Pigeon are worth noting—the greatest perhaps is High Falls, about two miles above the mouth of the river. This 120-foot cataract—and the other white water along this stretch of the Pigeon—was the reason for the establishment of Grand Portage, some 50 miles south.

Grand Portage is the name of the fort and trading post on the shore of Lake Superior, as well as the nine-mile hike voyageurs took to avoid the falls and rapids on the lower Pigeon. The stockade at Grand Portage has been restored, and the portage itself has been kept clear for access to Boundary Waters Canoe Area and the site of Fort Charlotte, on the Pigeon River.

All of Minnesota is watery country, and the Arrowhead, defined by water on the north and south, is also traversed by several rivers which drain into Lake Superior. North to south they are: Pigeon, Reservation, Arrowhead, Devil's Track, Cascade, Onion, Temperance, Two Island, Caribou, Manitou, Beaver, Knife and French. That is about one river for every ten miles. The streams vary in character, and all that can be said reliably about them as a group is that the fishing is good just about everywhere, and the rugged nature of the land promises many delights to the person who chooses to explore on foot.

Palisade Head is a must for travelers along the north shore. It's a granite headland rising more than 300 feet above the waters of the lake, its vaguely rose-colored walls stained with sea-green lichen which echoes the shade of the water. From the lookout point it's possible to see the Apostle Islands and the Wisconsin shoreline lurking in the distant mist, while the ever-present gulls dive and swoop above the surface of the lake. The early-morning visitor is likely to find the cliffs wrapped in the fog which hangs over the lake on cool mornings, concealed and then revealed as wispy clouds play hide and seek among the rugged headlands.

A few miles distant is another Minnesota landmark. Split Rock Lighthouse stands on the crown of a cliff overlooking dangerous offshore reefs. The warning of this sentinel was particularly valuable because of the magnetic rock hereabouts, which rendered ships' compasses useless. Beginning in 1909 the 370,000-candlepower light and the foghorn combined to warn lake traffic of the treacherous waters for fifty years. Now the venerable lighthouse is a state park.

(Following page, above) This peaceful lake scene is in the Boundary Waters Canoe Area in northern Minnesota.
(Following page, below) Birches lean out over a gravelly beach at Cutface Bay.

SOUTHERN MINNESOTA

The southern portion of Minnesota is one of the few parts of the state that can be accorded the status of a separate geographical region. Unlike the lakes-and-woods aspect of the rest of the state, southern Minnesota more closely resembles a continuation of the Iowa Corn Belt or the Great Plains—which it is. The nature of the land makes the nature of the economy different, as well: this is farming and dairy country.

For the sake of discussion, southern Minnesota can be divided into three areas, two of which have actual physical differences and a third one which lies in-between. In the east is the Hill Country, the only portion of Minnesota which did not have its hills and valleys rearranged by glaciers at one time or another. In the west lies Minnesota's share of the Great Plains. The middle is a transitional area which used to be the Big Woods.

Before the coming of the white man, there was forest almost without interruption from the Atlantic Ocean to the Mississippi River and beyond. In Minnesota all the land east of the Mississippi was forested, except for excessively swampy areas, and timbered land extended west of the river from 30 to 120 miles. One particular area, where the rainfall was adequate and the soil rich in lime, became known quite early as the Big Woods because of the incredible size of the indigenous hardwood trees. The Big Woods lay for the most part in the triangular area defined by St. Cloud, Mankato and Northfield.

To early settlers, the big trees meant only one thing: rich farmland underneath. They cleared the land as quickly as possible, usually by burning, sparing only those areas too rugged to farm. Nerstrand State Park preserves a stand of these magnificent hardwood trees today, and the term Big Woods is used in an historical sense only. Today, rich and productive farms dominate the area where the Big Woods was, and the place is drained by several scenic rivers.

The eastern tip of Minnesota offers some of the most varied scenery in the state. This land was never subjected to the bulldozing of glaciers, and it has a more rugged aspect as a result. The backroads of this portion of the state are a special treat for explorers and local history buffs: every secluded hamlet has a tale to tell to the person

(Preceding page) Early morning fog is nearly cleared from the St. Croix River in Interstate Park, in this view from the picnic area.

willing to take the time. Handsome, well-kept farms are the rule hereabouts, with a diversity of crops. Orchard crops have grown here since Territorial days, and special stock adapted to cold winters and short growing seasons has made this portion of Minnesota a leader in fruit production. Dairying is big business, and wheat and corn are grown as feed and as cash crops. Over to the west, where the land begins to smooth out a little, is the home of Minnesota's other giant: Le Seur is the birthplace of one of America's longest-lived trademarks: the Jolly Green Giant was born here in the 1920s.

One of the curiosities of the southern portion of Minnesota is a number of spectacular underground caverns, happy accidents of nature which are found where the magic ingredients of limestone and running water exist in the right proportions and there is a great deal of time. The proportions were just right in the Harmony-Spring Valley area, and some breathtaking underground scenery is the result. Niagara Cave, a few miles outside of Harmony, was discovered in the 1920s by a farmer whose pigs kept disappearing mysteriously. He found out where they were going when he located an opening to the cave, which has about five miles of passageways on three distinct levels, as well as an underground waterfall. There are incredible erosional features caused by the dripping water, which wears limestone away in one place, and deposits it in another.

As the traveler moves westward, the land begins to smooth out into the sweeping undulations of the plains. This was some of the last land settled in Minnesota. The Great Plains were labeled ''The Great American Desert'' on early maps, and nobody had any idea of the richness of the soil under that wind-rippled grass. Other parts of the state had timber, and rivers at their doorsteps, so it took a combination of railroads, cheap land via the Homestead Act, and a promising market in wheat to lure homesteaders out onto the prairies. Once the sod was broken, however, it didn't take long for Minnesota to rise to the top of the nation in wheat and flour production on the basis of this rich land, a position which was maintained until the 1920s.

To some people, the words ''prairie scenery'' are a contradiction in terms—they prefer lakes, mountains, rivers, trees . . . something to fill up all that space. Others write lyrically of vast prairies in terms that liken them to great seascapes, broad canvases in which the light, rather than a means to see other things, becomes something to look at in itself. Whatever the personal evaluation, it is clear that the Great Plains are built on a scale that makes human efforts seem small. No windbreak

(Following page) Devil's Kettle Falls, on the Brule River, divides at the top of the bluff. The right half plunges down the rocky face; the left half disappears into a huge pothole at the top of the rock face.

line of trees, no monolithic grain elevator can reach to the sky or move the horizon closer. Prairie people feel things closing in on them when they can't see out at least ten miles, while the valley dweller may start looking for something to hold on to in the midst of all that emptiness.

Happily, southern Minnesota has a little something to offer to everyone in terms of scenery. For instance, the Minnesota River loops through the south part of the state, turning north to join the Mississippi at Minneapolis. The Minnesota is the remnant of a prehistoric stream called the River Warren which flowed here when glaciers and their meltwaters were still rearranging the landscape. The Warren drained Lake Agassiz in the days when glacial ice blocked its northern outlet, cutting its deep, broad valley through the plains. When the ice melted in the north, Agassiz drained in that direction until nothing was left but the Red River, and the Minnesota was left to run southward in the valley of the mighty Warren. Other rivers, too, have scored the plains deeply, providing wooded canyons with striking waterfalls, and the sort of erosional wonder that can be seen at Pipestone National Monument, where Indians still mine the reddish stone for the manufacture of pipes.

Glaciers have also done their part to add some variety to the plains. The idea that the great icecaps primarily scraped things smooth and left them that way is contradicted by much of what can be seen in this country. It is true that a glacier carries a great deal of debris along with it, tending to grind down the high places and fill in the low ones. But where the glacier filled in existing valleys and riverbeds, a chain of lakes might be the result a few thousand years later when things warmed up. And as the big ice sheets melted, rubble they carried along was left lying about, helter-skelter, to become low ridges and gentle prairie hills. So while there's no mitigating the size of the sky, or altering the immense openness that comes with the prairie, there's considerable variety here for the person tuned to subtlety and grandeur on a very large scale.

(Preceding page, above) The Norway Brook Pine River slides quietly past trees tinged with the colors of October.

(Preceding page, below) Early morning sun bursts on the waters of the Mississippi River at its source on Lake Itasca.

Enlarged Prints

of most of the photography
in this book
are available.
Send self-addressed,
stamped envelope
for information.
Beautiful America Publishing Company
4720 S.W. Washington
Beaverton, Oregon 97005

(Following page) Spectacular sunsets are a way of life in Minnesota's Detroit Lakes area.